# Learn Spanish with

# BATMAN™

## Rogues Gallery

Writ... ...y:
Sco...
Dan... ...t
Ty T...

Col...
Lee...

...Guzman

Phil Felix

Contacting the Editors:
Every effort has been made to provide accurate
information in this publication, but changes are
inevitable. The publisher cannot be responsible
for any resulting loss, inconvenience or injury.
We would appreciate it if readers would call
our attention to any errors or outdated information.

Please contact us at:
Berlitz Publishing
193 Morris Avenue
Springfield, NJ 07081, USA.
E-mail: comments@berlitzbooks.com

Publishing Director: Sheryl Olinsky Borg
Editor/Project Manager: Emily Bernath
Senior Editor: Lorraine Sova
Editorial Assistant: Eric Zuarino
Interior Design: Claudia Petrilli, Doug Wolff
Production Manager: Elizabeth Gaynor
Cover Design: DC Comics & Claudia Petrilli

ESCUCHA, THIS ISN'T WHAT YOU THINK THIS TIME

IT NEVER IS, WITH YOU.

VALE.

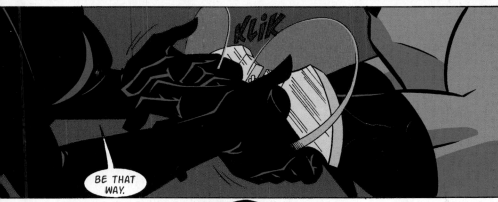

KLIK

BE THAT WAY.

YOU'RE NEVER WILLING TO JUST...

¡AH, OLVÍDALO!

escucha
listen

vale
fine

¡Ah, olvídalo!
Ah, forget it!

Perdóname, por favor.
Please excuse me.

¡Una bomba!
A bomb!

¿Qué haces?
What are you
doing?

bueno
well

sí
yes

escucha
listen

criminales
criminals

¡Dios mío!
Oh my God!

por favor
please

Y tú eres...
And you are...

tú
you

escucha
listen

en su vida
in her life

bueno
right

esa noche
that evening

allí
there

BUENO, HERE'S SOMETHING.

I, UH, LOOKED INTO DETECTIVE MONTOYA'S FILES... THERE'S BEEN NOTHING OFFICIALLY REPORTED, BUT A BUNCH OF RUMORS.

APPARENTLY THERE'S BEEN A RASH OF BURGLARIES LATELY BUT, FOR SOME REASON, THE VICTIMS AREN'T REPORTING THEM TO THE POLICE.

GIVE ME A NAME AND AN ADDRESS.

OKAY! ME LLAMO TODD AND VIVO EN--

NOT YOU.

bueno
okay

me llamo
my name is

vivo en
I live in

la luna
moon

el dinero
money

el fuego
fire

12

el auto
car

las escaleras
stairs

la luna
moon

13

alerta
alert

pequeña
small

14

YOU HAD SOME EXTRAORDINARILY EXPENSIVE ITEMS STOLEN RECENTLY. A PAIR OF PICASSOS. YET YOU DIDN'T REPORT IT.

¿POR QUÉ NO? A LITTLE INSURANCE FRAUD, QUIZÁS?

¡NO! NO ENTIENDES.

AFTER BRAGGING AT THE ICEBERG ABOUT FINALLY GETTING THE PICASSOS -- EVEN OUTBIDDING MAURIZIO FOR THEM --

HOW COULD I ADMIT THAT I, OF ALL PEOPLE, HAD BEEN ROBBED? SABES HOW HUMILIATING IT IS TO FIND YOUR SECURITY IS...

...WORTHLESS?

THE ICEBERG? QUIERES DECIR THE ICEBERG LOUNGE?

CLARO.

DON'T TELL ANYONE THERE, POR FAVOR.

¿Por qué no?
Why not?

quizás
maybe

¡No!
No!

no entiendes
you don't
understand

sabes
do you know

quieres decir
do you mean

claro
of course

por favor
please

vamos a ver
let's see

y
and

sí
yes

16

la luna
moon

la luz
light

el gato
cat

bueno
well

mensaje
message

bueno
well

vidas
lives

una historia
a story

dónde y cuándo
hacerlo
where and when
to do it

19

tienes razón
you're right

se acabó
it's over

vidas
lives

SO IT SEEMS THERE'S BEEN A CORRESPONDING NUMBER OF LARGE, ANONYMOUS DONATIONS TO VARIOUS ANIMAL-RIGHTS GROUPS.

*PARECE QUE* CATWOMAN'S BEEN DOING THE ROBIN HOOD THING. MAYBE SHE'S TURNING OVER A NEW LEAF.

SHE'S A THIEF.

*MIRA*, SHE RIPPED OFF PEOPLE WITH MAFIA CONNECTIONS, AND SHE DIDN'T KEEP THE MONEY. SHE USED IT TO DO GOOD.

*ESO NO IMPORTA.* SHE'S STILL *UNA CRIMINAL.*

YEAH...AND THE WAY YOU VISITED BORODIN EARLIER? SOME WOULD CALL THAT BREAKING AND ENTERING. THAT MAKES YOU A FELON.

ANYWAY, WHY ARE YOU SO MUCH TOUGHER ON HER THAN YOU ARE ON, SAY, TWO-FACE?

YOU ALWAYS HOLD OUT HOPE THAT HE CAN BE RE-HABILITATED. SO WHY SO HARD ON CATWOMAN?

*PORQUE* I EXPECT MORE FROM HER.

parece que
looks like

mira
look

eso no importa
it doesn't matter

una criminal
a criminal

porque
because

bueno, pues
yeah, well

escucha
Listen

está bien
that's fine

pero
but

la luna
moon

el gato
cat

la comida
food

23

anoche
last night

¿Agua?
Water?

escucha
listen

gracias
thank you

de nada
you're welcome

no más
no more

ahora
now

¿Qué es eso?
What's that?

¿Alo?
Hello?

parece que
it looks like

nada
nothing

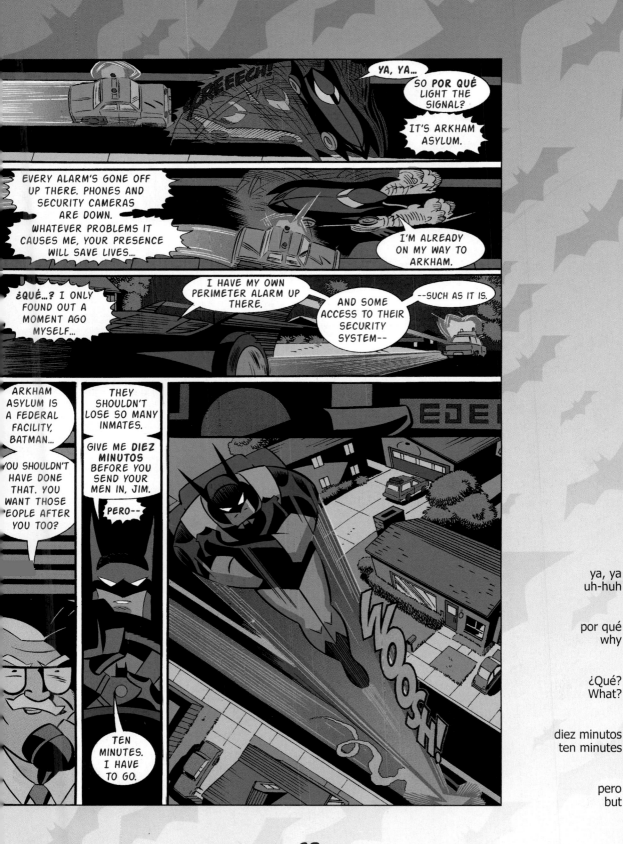

ya, ya
uh-huh

por qué
why

¿Qué?
What?

diez minutos
ten minutes

pero
but

corran
run

muévete
move it

oh Dios
oh God

¿Necesitas ayuda?
Do you need help?

no, gracias
no thank you

no necesito ayuda
I don't need help

ahora
now

28

sí
yes

qué bueno
that's good

estupendo
splendid

no
no

directo a casa,
entonces
straight home, then

¡Quiero salir!
I want to get out!

esto está bien
this is good

mala suerte
bad luck

pero
but

un minuto
a minute

la primera
the first

quiero salir
I want to get out

allí
over there

quiero salir
I want to get out

hombres
men

un hombre
a man

estás viva
you're alive

¿Cómo?
How?

34

quiero salir
I want to get out

¿Estás bien?
Are you okay?

la bomba
the bomb

¿Dónde está?
Where is it?

¿Me puedes ayudar?
Could you help me?

por favor
please

en un minuto
in a minute

37

manos
hands

gracias
thanks

¿Estas bien?
Are you okay?

hace dos segundos
two seconds ago

¡Mira!
Look!

por supuesto
of course

mira
look

la luz
the light

dónde están
where are

mensaje
message

41

la película
the movie

mi favorito
my favorite

caballero
gentleman

un héroe
a hero

mi vida
my life

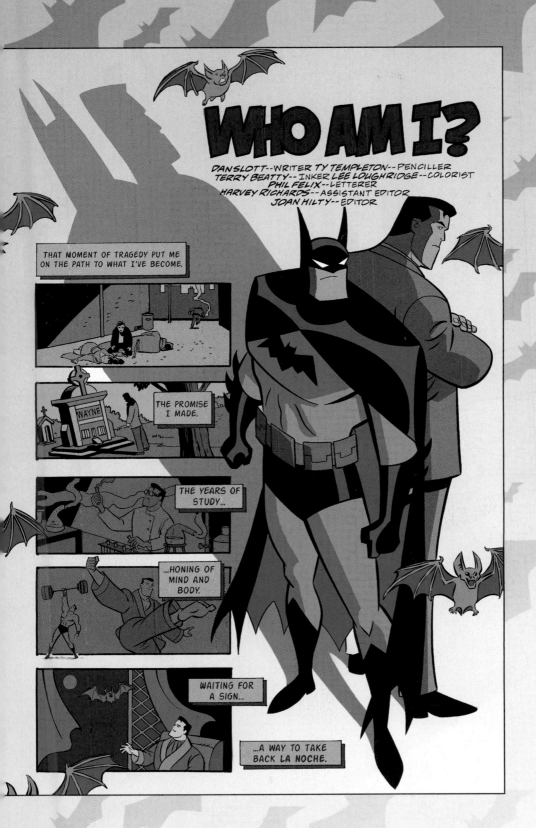

# WHO AM I?

DAN SLOTT--WRITER TY TEMPLETON--PENCILLER
TERRY BEATTY--INKER LEE LOUGHRIDGE--COLORIST
PHIL FELIX--LETTERER
HARVEY RICHARDS--ASSISTANT EDITOR
JOAN HILTY--EDITOR

THAT MOMENT OF TRAGEDY PUT ME ON THE PATH TO WHAT I'VE BECOME.

THE PROMISE I MADE.

THE YEARS OF STUDY...

...HONING OF MIND AND BODY.

WAITING FOR A SIGN...

...A WAY TO TAKE BACK LA NOCHE.

la noche
the night

¡Lo prometo!
I promise!

bueno
well

algo
something

mira
look

bien hecho
well done

y otra vez
and again

y una cosa más
and one more thing

46

ricos
rich

sabes
you know

quiero decir
I mean

del mundo
in the world

cállate
be quiet

todo el mundo
everybody

excepto tú
except you

¿Quién eres tú?
Who are you?

nadie
nobody

pero
but

es difícil
it's hard

está en todas partes
he's everywhere

no me molesta
it doesn't bother me

bueno
well

por qué
why

primera pelea
first fight

alguien
someone

¡Socorro!
Help!

entonces
so

¿Dónde estoy?
Where am I?

¡Rápido!
Hurry!

¿Qué era eso?
What was that?

¿Alo?
Hello?

entiendo
I understand

lo siento
I'm sorry

¿Quién eres?
Who are you?

¿Qué está pasando?
What's going on?

¡Ay, Dios mio!
Oh my God!

cállate
shut up

ahora mismo
right now

un hombre
a man

algo
something

56

PERO...BUT I'M NOT AN "UNDERWORLD FIGURE" ANYMORE! I'M CURED! I'M A FREE MAN.

CURED?

"THE MEDIUM IS THE MESSAGE." YOU BROADCAST YOUR RIDDLE OF THE MEDIUM ON TELEVISION...SO THE "MOO-SEUM" OF YOUR RIDDLE WAS THE MUSEUM OF TELEVISION BROADCASTING.

YES, YOU SOLVED IT, LO SÉ...YOU'RE HERE!

WHY NOT JUST SAY WHERE YOU WERE? WHY GAMBLE YOUR LIFE ON THE RIDDLE?

OH, I WASN'T GAMBLING, BATMAN!

LEAVE IT TO GOPHE[...]

SMOKING GUNS

YOUR LUCKY DAY

IT WAS AN EASY ONE...

...I KNEW YOU'D GET IT.

I DON'T HAVE TIME FOR GAMES, RIDDLER. FIND ANOTHER PLAYMATE.

¿EN SERIO? THERE'S STILL ANOTHER KILLER AFTER ME...AREN'T YOU GOING TO HELP?

HERE'S A RIDDLE...

WHY SHOULD I?

pero
but

lo sé
I know

en serio
seriously

además
also

¿Cómo?
How?

pero
but

No. No puedes.
No you cannot.

58

Pero ¿dónde?
But where?

¡Olvida eso!
Forget it!

mi vida
my life

todo el mundo
everybody

un idiota
an idiot

60

los ojos
eyes

las orejas
ears

la mano
hand

las piernas
legs

ya veremos
we'll see

por ahora
for now

nada más
nothing more

espera un minuto
wait a minute

ahora
now

eres enfermo
you're sick

un hombre libre
a free man

trabajo duro
hard work

ciudad
city

también
also

BACK TO THE OFFICE, MR. STORK!

IT'S A BUSY *DÍA*, AND THERE'S STILL MUCH TO DO.

RIGHT-O, BOSS.

MR. MAYOR? MAY I, SIR?

GRACIAS, *SEÑORITA* PARTRIDGE. YOU KNOW WHAT I STILL CAN'T GET OVER, MY DEAR?

THAT THEY ACTUALLY PAY ME FOR THIS.

WAUGH-WA-WA!

MISTAH MAYOR...

*AHORA NO, SEÑORITA* PEACOCK. JUST BE A DEAR AND HOLD MY CALLS. I DON'T WISH TO BE DISTURBED FOR A WHILE.

BUT MAYOR COBBLEPOT, DERE'S SOME GENTLEMENS HERE TA SEE YOU...

PENGUIN. NICE DESK.

!

SURELY YOU HAVE SOME TIME FOR...

...YOUR *VIEJO AMIGO*, RUPERT THORNE?

día
day

gracias
thank you

señorita
Miss

ahora no
not now

viejo amigo
old friend

65

señorita
Miss

por favor
please

sí señor
yes sir

de hecho
actually

alguien
someone

un trato
a deal

por supuesto
of course

sí señor
yes sir

policía de Gotham
Gotham police

vida
life

dinero
money

¡Dios mio!
My God

buen trabajo
good work

muy bien
very well

quizás
maybe

cielo
sweetie

ojos
eyes

¿No entiendes?
Don't you get it?

está bien
it's ok

olvídalo
forget it

¿Qué?
What?

rosas
roses

piensa rápido
think fast

cariño
baby

no...tienes razón
no...you're right

alguien
someone

claro
of course

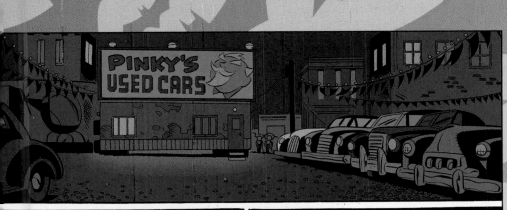

TAPPA TAPPA TAP TAP

PINKY MCCONNEL?

AHH!

BATMAN!

...BUT TO ADVERTISE "THE JOKER'S HELICOPTER" FOR SALE ON E-BUY...THAT'S JUST ESTÚPIDO.

DO YOU KNOW WHAT IT'S WORTH?

IS IT WORTH YOUR LIFE?

BAD ENOUGH THAT YOU DO BUSINESS WITH A CRIMINAL MADMAN LIKE THE JOKER...

EL AÑO PASADO, I SOLD MATT HAGEN'S BEAT-UP OLD BUICK FOR FIFTY THOUSAND DÓLARES! THERE ARE COLLECTORS OUT THERE—

HOW MUCH DID JOKER PAY YOU? ¿DÓNDE ESTÁ?

estúpido
stupid

el año pasado
last year

dólares
dollars

¿Dónde está?
Where is he?

YOU KNOW WHERE HE IS.

I DON'T HAVE TO TELL YOU ANYTHING...

...YOU'RE A WANTED MAN.

I EVEN HEARD OUR MAYOR'S GOT A PRICE ON YOUR HEAD.

SIÉNTATE AND START TALKING

KLIK!

BLAM!

...AT THE CITY PRISON WHERE INMATES HAVE BEEN HOUSED FOLLOWING AN EXPLOSION AT ARKHAM ASYLUM, THERE HAS BEEN ANOTHER ESCAPE.

. HERE'S CAPTAIN RENEE MONTOYA OF THE GOTHAM MAJOR CRIMES UNIT.

WE'RE STILL ASSESSING THE SITUATION HERE, SUMMER, BUT THE ATTACK SEEMED AIMED AT BREAKING OUT THE CAPTURED ASSASSIN FROM THE ARKHAM INCIDENT...

siéntate
sit down

vale
okay

lo que tú digas
whatever you say

¿Qué quieres?
What do you want?

bueno
well

probablemente no
probably not

no te preocupes
cariño
don't worry baby

dinero
money

tu vida
your life

si no
if not

76

allí
there

difícil
difficult

ya sabes
you know that

difícil
difficult

patético
pathetic

BATMAN! ¡COLEGA! THIS IS BETTER THAN A BIRTHDAY!

DETECTIVE! WHEN LAST YOU FACED ME AT ARKHAM...YOU DID NOT FACE ME AT ALL.

INSTEAD YOU ATTACKED ME FROM BEHIND.

THIS SHOULD PROVE **INTERESANTE**. I HAVE SUFFERED THROUGH MANY LONG TALES OF YOUR PHYSICAL PROWESS.

DO YOU DARE FACE ME **AHORA**--MAN TO MAN?

BUT I AM MASTER OF FIVE DISCIPLINES.

LET'S PUT IT TO A TEST.

colega
buddy

ahora
now

interesante
interesting

79

mi ciudad
my city

sus juegos
his games

cielo
sweetie

un hombre
man

orejas
ears

¿Qué?
What?

bueno
well

orejas
ears

mira eso
look at that

¡Uy, qué miedo!
I'm so scared!

ahora no
not now

83

fallaste
you missed

mírame
look at me

adios
bye

no soy un criminal
I'm not a criminal

genial
great

un segundo
wait a sec

sí
yeah

86

ya se acabó
it's over

veneno
poison

¿Dónde estoy?
Where am I?

emergencia
emergency

está en peligro
is in danger

todo
everything

cuidado
careful

parece que
looks like

¿Qué?
What?

se están riendo
they're laughing

oxígeno
oxygen

¿No es genial?
Isn't this great?

¿No lo entiendes?
Don't you get it?

90

ese, ahí
that one, over there

ahora
now

tu propia vida
your own life

años
years

nunca
never

y lo hice
and I did it

¿Qué?
What?

dónde está
where is

dos veces
twice

un cobarde
coward

tengo razón
I'm right

vida
life

un cobarde
a coward

gracias
thank you

yo soy
I am

nada
nothing

computadora
computer

completo
complete

ahí está
there it is

no
no

nos vemos
see you around

estoy lista
I'm ready

ah, sí
ah, yes

conozco
I recognize

claro que
of course

pero
but

¿Por qué?
Why?

EASTER ISLAND, IN THE SOUTH PACIFIC...

SUNDOWN.

SONOGRAM CONFIRMS IT.

THIS MOAI STATUE IS HOLLOW. AND DIRECTLY OVER AN UNDERGROUND CHAMBER.

I'VE GOT A SEAM RUNNING BELOW THE ROCK FACE... IT GOES...

KLIK!

ALLÍ. I'VE TRIPPED A SECRET OPENING... VOY A ENTRAR.

YOU'VE PROBABLY TRIPPED A DOZEN ALARMS AS WELL. I COULD BE MORE HELP TO YOU ON THE GROUND INSTEAD OF FLYING THE BAT-TAXI.

NO. IAN.

RA'S AL GHUL IS THE MOST RUTH- LESS MAN ALIVE, ROBIN. YOU DON'T FACE HIM.

YOU HOVER AND WAIT FOR INSTRUCCIONES.

allí
there

voy a entrar
I'm going in

instrucciones
instructions

97

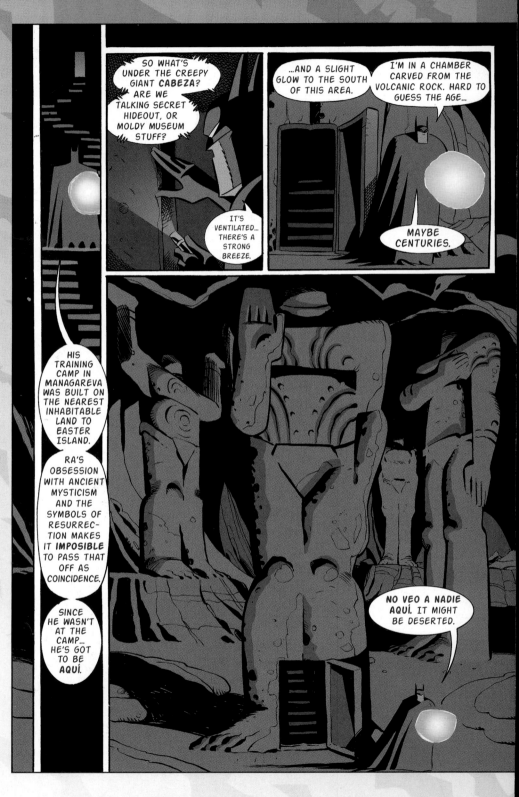

imposible
impossible

aquí
here

cabeza
head

no veo a nadie aquí
I don't see anybody here

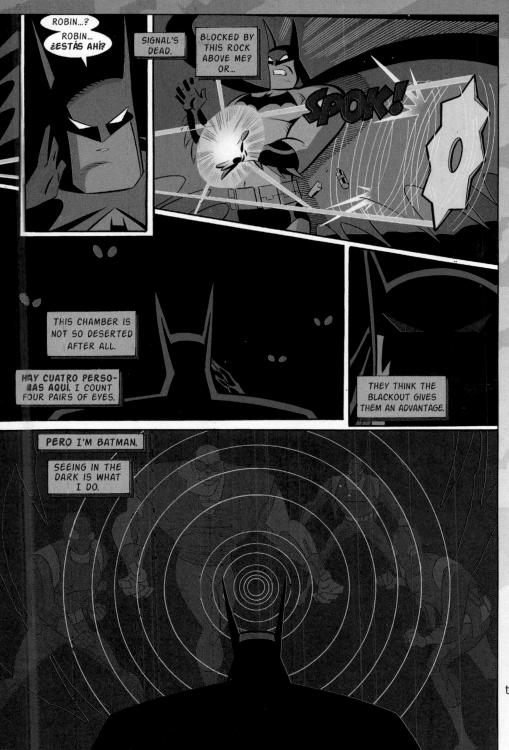

¿Estás ahí?
Are you there?

hay cuatro personas
aquí
there are four people
here

pero
but

hay alguien más aquí
there's someone else
here

rosas
roses

mi padre y tú
my father and you

THE UNMISTAKABLE SMELL OF ROTTING MEAT AND JASMINE WAKES ME.

ONE OF THE MYSTERIOUS HEALING POOLS IN WHICH RA'S AL GHUL IMMERSES HIMSELF IN ORDER TO REMAIN IMMORTAL.

THESE PITS HAVE KEPT HIM ALIVE FOR CENTURIES--PERO TAMBIÉN THEY DROVE HIM MAD.

I'M NEAR A LAZARUS PIT.

RAPA NUI IS SACRED TO ME, DETECTIVE.

I'VE RETURNED HERE OFTEN SINCE MY AÑOS WITH CAPTAIN COOK AND THE BRITISH NAVY...

THIS TRAGIC ISLAND IS NEVER FAR FROM MY THOUGHTS.

PERO, ¿POR QUÉ ESTÁ USTED AQUÍ? WHY NOW?

BECAUSE YOU WEREN'T AT YOUR BASE ON MANGAREVA.

YOU SENT SHADOW ASSASSINS FROM THERE TO GOTHAM. TRIED TO KILL JOKER, TWO-FACE, POISON IVY, RIDDLER...

ARE YOU MOVING INTO GOTHAM AND ELIMINATING THE COMPETITION?

NO.

I'M AMAZED YOU DISCOVERED THAT INSTALLATION. NO DOUBT THAT'S WHY WE LOST CONTACT WITH THEM...

¿POR QUÉ?

SETTLING A VENDETTA?

NO.

pero también
but also

años
years

pero
but

¿Por qué está usted aquí?
Why are you here?

¿Por qué?
Why?

no
no

era un regalo
it was a gift

absolutamente
absolutely

mi hija
my daughter

tú eres muy
importante
you are very
important

pero
but

simplemente eso
simply that

¡BASTA YA!

NO ONE DIES FOR ME!

VAMOS, BRUCE. YOU'VE NEVER WISHED THEM DEAD...EVEN FOR JUST A MOMENT?

MY FATHER OFFERS TO SOLVE ALL YOUR PROBLEMS...

AND YOU GET TO KEEP THE BLOOD AWAY FROM YOUR HANDS.

YOU AND I CAN FINALLY FIND THE TIME TO--

TALIA... ESTÁS EN-FERMA. AS SICK AS HE IS.

BELOVED...?

¿PUEDES PONERTE DE PIE? THE POTION IN THAT DART--

...WAS AN OLD FORMULA I'VE FOUND AN ANTITOXIN FOR MONTHS AGO.

RA'S-- I'VE HAD IT WITH YOU PLAYING GOD!

¿QUÉ...?

¡Basta ya!
Enough!

vamos
come on

estás enferma
you're sick

¿Puedes ponerte
de pie?
Can you stand?

¿Qué?
What?

103

¿Para qué?
For what?

porque
because

ridículo
ridiculous

hija
daughter

no
no

y lo sabes
and you know it

hombres
men

vale, sin juegos
ok, no games

la hija
the daughter

¿Eso importa?
Does it matter?

para
stop

cobardes
cowards

hija
daughter

ten cuidado
be careful

soy tu padre
I am your father

por favor
please

me pregunto
I wonder

MY LEGS GIVE OUT FOR A SECOND.

I HOPE RA'S IS IN WORSE SHAPE.

¿PUEDES MOVERTE?

BARELY...

YOU DIDN'T FIGHT BACK.

ES MI HIJA.

I COULD NO MORE RAISE MY HAND TO HARM HER...

...THAN YOU COULD.

YOU WOULD NOT HAVE ME DEFENSELESS LIKE THIS IF NOT FOR HER...

I'D HAVE FOUND A WAY.

BUT TO DO THIS.

TO USE HER SHAMEFUL MOMENT OF MADNESS TO YOUR ADVANTAGE IN THIS GAME WE PLAY... NO TE VA A PERDONAR.

MURDER IS NOT UN JUEGO, RA'S--

AND YOU'RE NOT ESCAPING JUSTICE ANYMORE.

¿Puedes moverte?
Can you move?

es mi hija
she is my daughter

no te va a perdonar
she won't forgive you

un juego
a game

110

¡Cuidado, eso duele!
Careful, that hurts!

mi hija
my daughter

¿Está bien?
Is she all right?

está bien
she's all right

justicia
justice

¿Dónde está mi
padre?
Where is my father?

no lo sé
I don't know

tenemos que irnos
we need to leave

no hay mensajes
there are no
messages